Think. Learn. Compute.

This workbook was designed with kids in mind. It was tailored to help children build a strong foundation in the area of computer science. It is filled with practice pages and activities to maximize fun through learning.

This book belongs to:

_____

Computer Science Workbook

Think. Learn. Compute.

ISBN 9781521048306
Printed in U.S.A

TABLE OF CONTENTS

What is a Computer? 5

Computer Lab Rules 6

Computer Input Devices

Keyboard 8

Mouse 9

Scanner 10

Microphone 11

Joystick 12

Input Device Word Search 13

Input Device Maze 14

Cut and Paste Exercise 15

Drawing Exercise 16

Types of Computers

Personal Computer 18

Laptop Computer 19

Supercomputer 20

Microcomputer 21

Tablet Computer 22

PDA (Personal Digital Assistant) 23

Types of Computers Word Search 24

Types of Computers Maze 25

Drawing Exercise 26

History of Computers

Abacus 28

Pascaline 29

Stepped Reckoner 30

Jacquard Loom 31

Difference Engine 32

History of Computers Word Search 33

History of Computers Maze 34

Computer Output Devices

Monitor 36

Projector 37

Printer 38

Speaker 39

Output Device Review .... 40 – 41

Output Device Word Search 42

Output Device Maze 43

Drawing Exercise 44

TABLE OF CONTENTS

Storage Devices

Types of Storage Devices 46

Floppy Disk 47

CD-ROM 48

Flash Drive 49

Memory Card 50

Storage Devices Word Search 51

Storage Device Maze 52

Microsoft Office

Microsoft Office Software 54

Microsoft Word Home Tab 55-56

MS Home Tab – Open Icon 57

MS Home Tab – Save Icon 58

MS Home Tab – Cut Icon 59

MS Home Tab – Copy Icon 60

MS Home Tab – Paste Icon 61

Microsoft Office Word Search 62

Processing Device

CPU 64

Processing Device Word Search 65

Processing Device Maze 66

Glossary .... 67 - 70

References 71

What is a computer?

A computer is an electronic device, that can store and process data.

Computer Lab Rules

✓ DO NOT BRING FOOD OR DRINK INTO THE COMPUTER LAB.

✓ COME IN AND SIT DOWN QUIETLY.

✓ DO NOT PUSH ANY OBJECTS INTO COMPUTER OUTLETS.

✓ DO NOT TOUCH THE COMPUTER WITHOUT YOUR TEACHER'S PERMISSION.

✓ TIDY UP YOUR AREA BEFORE YOU LEAVE.

✓ PRINT ONLY WITH PERMISSION.

Computer Input Devices

Devices

Unit 1

Name: _____ Date: _____

Computer Keyboard

A computer **keyboard** is a board of keys, it has letters, numbers, symbols and special function keys on it.

Color the home row keys on the left **red.**
Color the home row keys on the right **blue**.
Color the spacebar key **purple.**
Color the enter key **orange.**

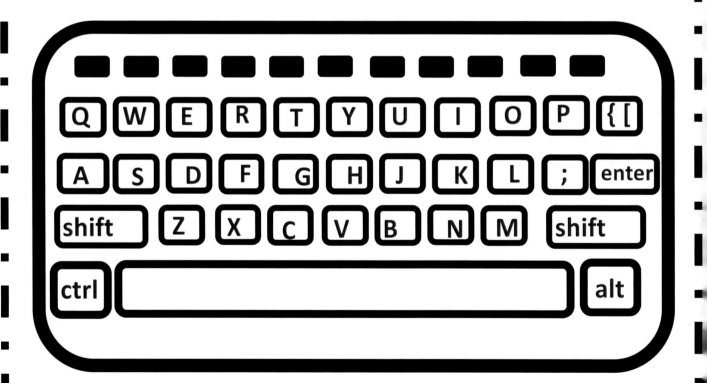

Computer Mouse

A **mouse,** is a small handheld device that has buttons that are used to click, double click and drag objects on the computer screen.

Color the left button - **green**, right button **red**, scroll wheel – **yellow**, and the body – **blue.**

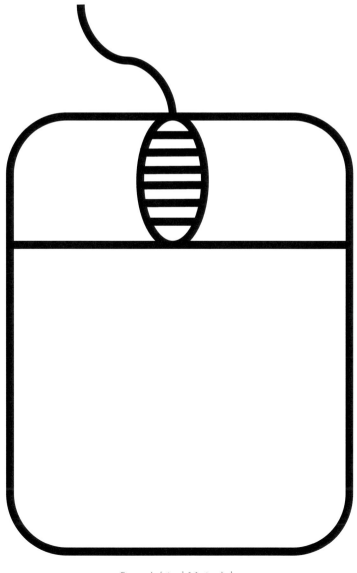

Name: _____ Date: _____

Computer Scanner

A **scanner** allows you to take a picture, drawing, or document (hard copy) and convert it into a file so that it can be stored on a computer.

Color the computer scanner below.

Name: _____ Date: _____

Computer Microphone

A **microphone** is a input device that allows you to input audio into your computer.

Color the picture of the microphone below.

Name: _____ Date: _____

Computer Joystick

A **joystick** is an input device that allows you to control a character or machine in a computer program.

Color the picture of the joystick below.

Name: _____ Date: _____

Computer Basic Parts

Use the word search puzzle to find the words listed below.

```
N  S  R  E  K  A  E  P  S  Y
P  S  R  E  T  N  I  R  P  P
Q  J  D  O  R  V  Y  R  J  T
F  E  E  L  E  I  G  E  Q  E
I  S  V  W  T  X  Z  S  N  J
Q  U  I  S  U  L  N  A  N  K
O  O  C  R  P  E  E  L  U  N
M  M  E  I  M  H  R  H  H  I
Z  D  R  A  O  B  Y  E  K  P
B  I  U  P  C  M  B  V  W  F
```

MOUSE   **COMPUTER**   **PRINTER**
CPU   **SPEAKERS**   **KEYBOARD**
INKJET   **PAIRS**   **LASER**

Name: _____ Date: _____

Computer Hardware Maze

Can you help Jake find his computer mouse?

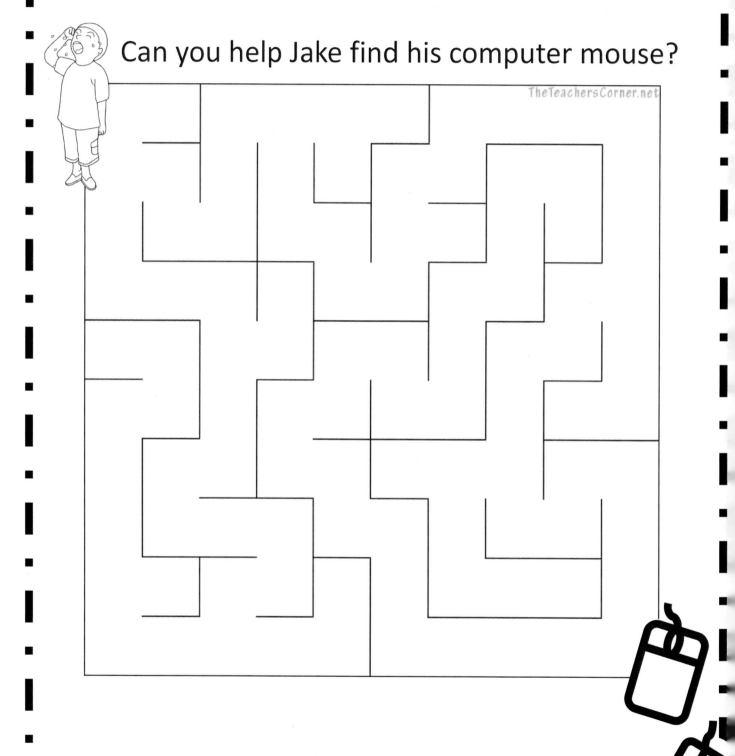

Name: _____ Date: _____

Computer Input Devices

Cut-out and paste a picture of each device listed below.

Wireless Mouse	Scanner
Microphone	**Monitor**

Computer Input Devices

Draw a picture of your favorite computer input device in the space provided below.

Types of Computers Unit 2

Name: _____ Date: _____

Personal Computer

A personal computer is a computer, created to be used by one person and is usually placed on a desk or table.

Color the picture of the Personal Computer below.

Name: _____ Date: _____

Laptop Computer

A **Laptop** computer has most, or all, of the same abilities as a desktop, but is small enough for you to carry around.

Color the picture of the laptop computer below.

Name: _____   Date: _____

Supercomputer

A **Supercomputer** is an array of computers that act as one collective machine capable of processing large amounts of data.

Color the picture of the Supercomputer below.

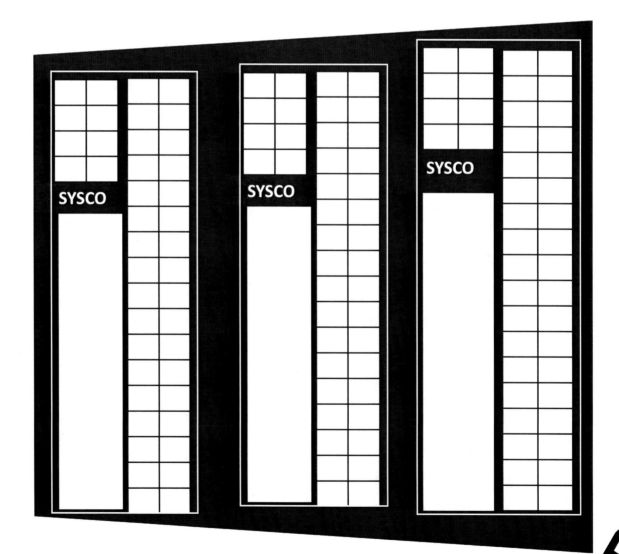

Name: _____ Date: _____

Minicomputer

A **minicomputer** is a Mid-sized computer that fits between microcomputers and mainframes or servers.

Color the picture of the minicomputer below.

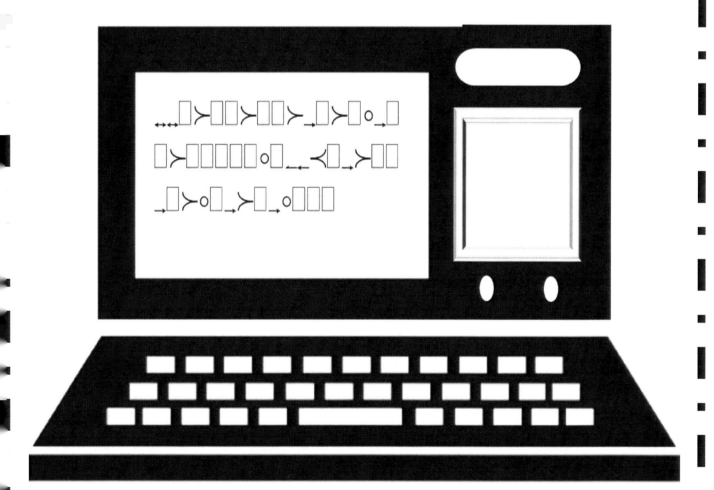

Name: _____ Date: _____

Tablet Computer

A **tablet** is a flat, portable computer with a touchscreen.

Color the picture of the Tablet computer below.

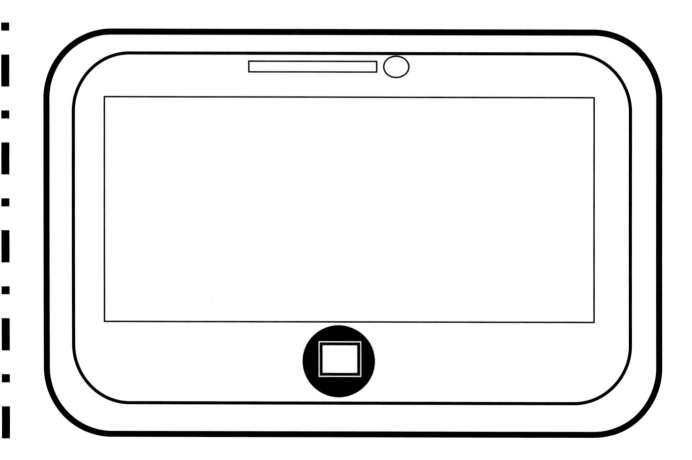

Name: _____ Date: _____

<u>PDA (Personal Digital Assistant)</u>

A **Personal Digital Assistant**, **PDA** is a little computer that fits in the palm of your hand.

Color the picture of the PDA computer below.

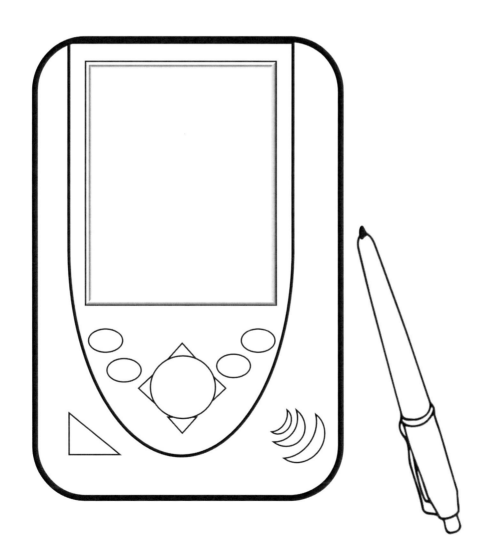

Types of Computers Word Search

```
R  D  W  G  B  B  P  G  E  Q
L  A  N  O  S  R  E  P  C  F
M  I  C  R  O  R  E  P  U  S
P  D  L  E  G  L  N  B  W  Z
P  C  A  T  E  L  B  A  T  A
K  X  P  U  X  Z  Z  T  J  D
L  Q  T  P  J  S  W  U  A  P
T  V  O  M  Q  V  J  Z  O  K
H  S  P  O  U  U  T  A  V  F
Z  O  S  C  Y  D  F  W  L  X
```

PERSONAL   **PDA**   **MICRO**

SUPER   **LAPTOP**   **TABLET**

Name: _____ Date: _____

Types of Computers Maze

Can you help Miney Mouse find her laptop computer?

TheTeachersCorner.net

Name: _____ Date: _____

Types of Computers

Draw a picture of your favorite type of computer in the space provided below.

History of Computers
Unit 3

Name: _____ Date: _____

The Abacus

The **Abacus** was created by the Babylonians around 300 B.C. It is the first known calculating machine used for counting.

Name: _____ Date: _____

The Pascaline

Pascaline is a calculating machine developed by Blaise Pascal in 1642.

The Stepped Reckoner

German Gottfried Wilhelm Leibniz invented the **Stepped Reckoner** in 1694. It could do addition, subtraction, multiplication, and division.

Name: _____ Date: _____

Jacquard Loom

The **Jacquard Loom** is a mechanical loom, invented by Joseph Marie Jacquard in 1801.

31

Name: _____ Date: _____

Difference Engine

The **Difference Engine** is a mechanical calculator first developed by Charles Babbage in 1822. Babbage is called the father of today's computers.

History of Computers Word Search

```
N  G  U  G  D  U  N  E  F  A
S  E  A  V  I  T  K  D  L  B
N  N  K  R  F  E  L  E  D  A
L  I  C  E  F  N  O  P  R  C
N  L  P  C  E  G  O  P  A  U
J  A  N  K  R  I  M  E  U  S
J  C  L  O  E  N  F  T  Q  I
V  S  X  N  N  E  Y  S  C  N
M  A  V  E  C  J  J  J  A  B
P  P  P  R  E  N  S  F  J  T
```

JACQUARD	**LOOM**	**STEPPED**
RECKONER	**ABACUS**	**PASCALINE**

Name: _____ Date: _____

History of Computers Maze

Can you help Blaise Pascal find his Pascaline Machine?

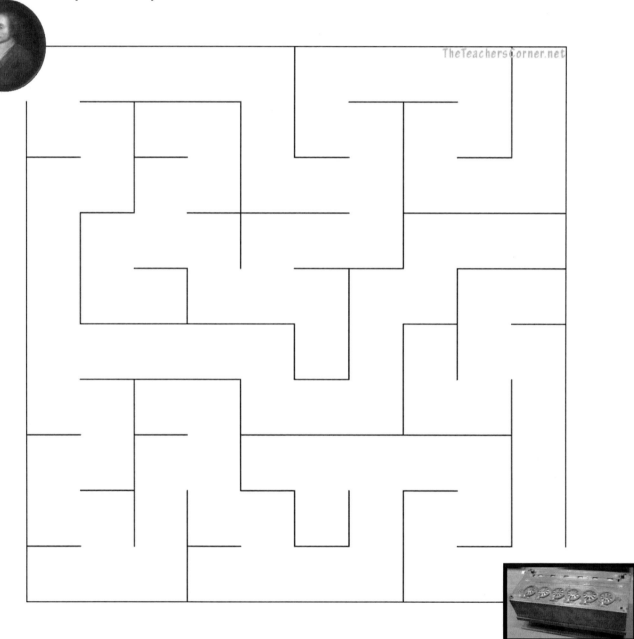

TheTeachersCorner.net

Computer Output Devices Unit 4

Name: _____ Date: _____

Computer Monitor

A computer monitor displays your work on the screen.

Color the computer monitor below.

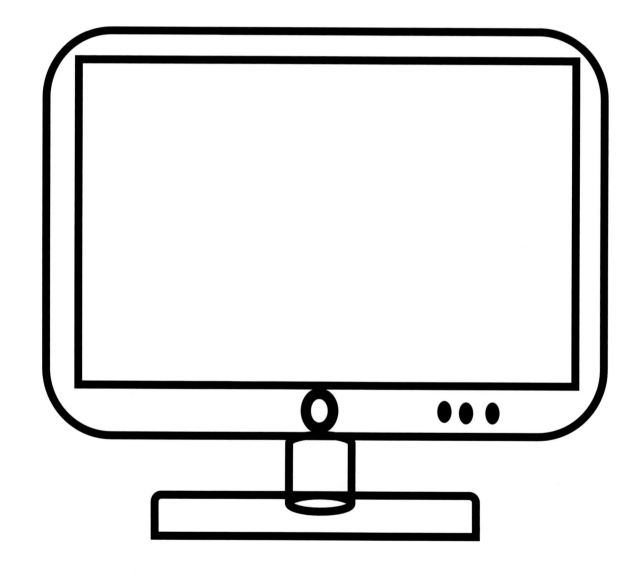

Name: _____ Date: _____

Projector

A **projector** can take images made on a computer and display them onto a large, flat, lightly colored surface.

Color the picture of the projector below.

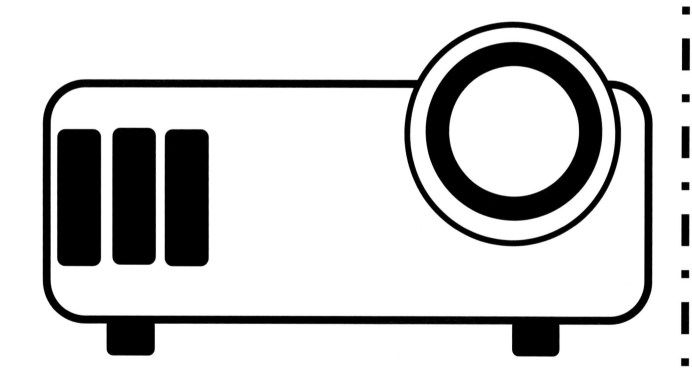

Name: _____ Date: _____

Printer

A **printer** is an output device that provides you with a paper copy of your work from a computer.

Color the printer below.

Name: _____ Date: _____

Computer Speakers

Speakers are output devices used with computer systems. Speakers usually come in pairs, which allows them to produce stereo sound.

Color the computer speakers below.

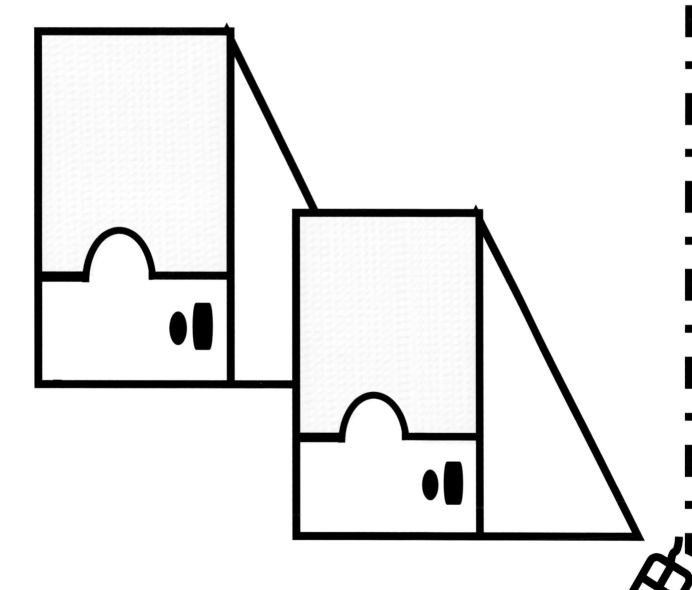

Name: _____ Date: _____

Computer Output Devices

Cut and Paste a picture of someone using the following output devices.

a. Printer

b. Monitor

Name: _____ Date: _____

Computer Output Devices

Write "T" is the statement is true and "F" is the statement is false next to each sentence.

1. Computer speakers are ONLY sold in pairs. _____

2. A printer is used to type letters. _____

3. A computer monitor lets you see your work. _____

4. A projector prints your work. _____

5. Computer speakers allow you to hear sound._____

Output Devices Word Search

K H E P P W G R H Z

K S R E K A E P S X

M P R I N T E R N P

U R J T X I A R M W

L R J G Q A W O M B

F R O T C E J O R P

L F M O N I T O R L

D M Z C J R H D A B

S E N O H P D A E H

D G H B G D H V S M

PRINTER **SPEAKERS** **MONITOR**

PROJECTOR **HEADPHONES**

Name: _____ Date: _____

Computer Output Devices Maze

Can you help Miney Mouse find her printer?

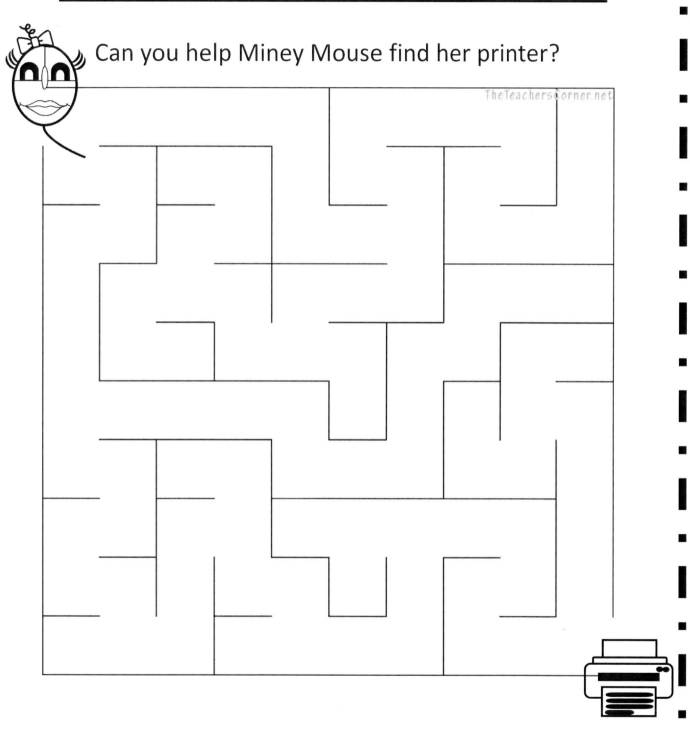

Name: _____ Date: _____

Computer Output Devices

Draw a picture of your favorite output device in the space provided below.

Computer Storage Devices

Unit 5

Name: _____ Date: _____

Types of Computer Storage

➢Primary Storage

➢Secondary Storage

➢Offline Storage

Name: _____ Date: _____

Storage Device-Floppy diskette

A **Floppy diskette** is a flexible removable magnetic disk used for storing data.

Color the picture of the floppy diskette below.

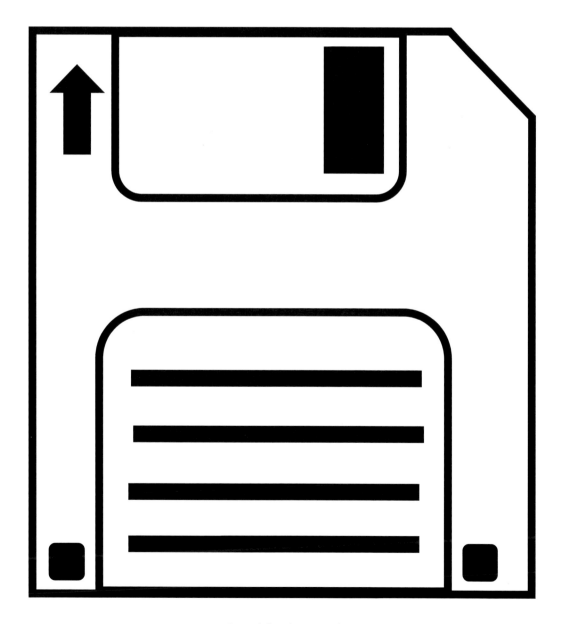

Storage Device – CD-Rom disc

A **CD-ROM** is a compact disc used as a read-only optical memory device.

Color the picture of the cd-rom disc below.

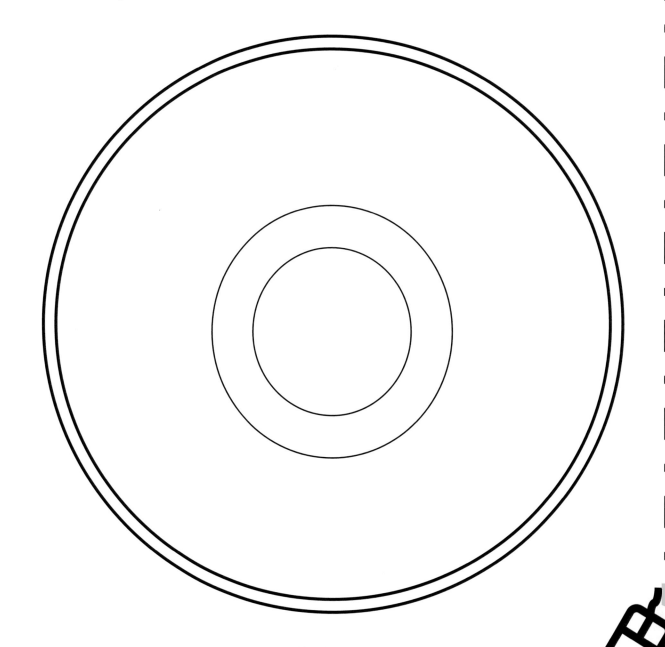

Name: _____ Date: _____

Storage Device – Flash Drive

A **flash drive** is a portable storage device that connects to a computer through a USB port.

Color the picture of the flash drive below.

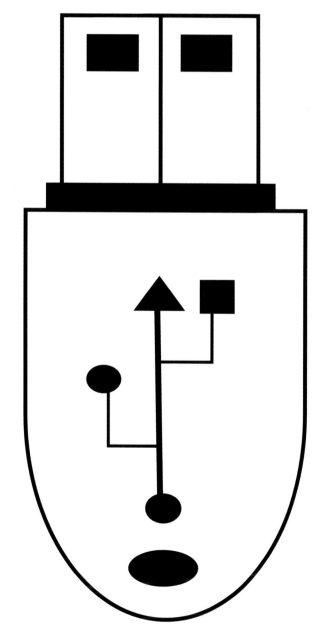

Name: _____ Date: _____

Storage Device – Memory Card

A memory card is a storage device that is often used to store photos and videos in electronic devices.

Color the picture of the memory card below.

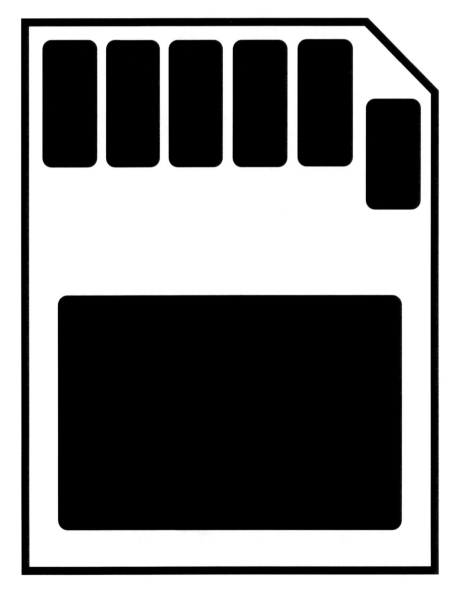

Name: _____ Date: _____

Storage Devices Word Search

W C D R O M R S M Z

A Z Y S R U C N F H

B D R P C S G M S D

S O O T P J O A F R

B L M M S O L N B A

L O E V Y F L J O C

A T M V W H F F I C

D D H L G Z Q R Z A

E G A R O T S D H Z

F Z S K O I B L A Y

STORAGE   **FLOPPY**   **MEMORY**

CARD   **CDROM**   **FLASH**

Name: _____ Date: _____

Computer Output Devices Maze

Can you help Miney Mouse find her Flash drive?

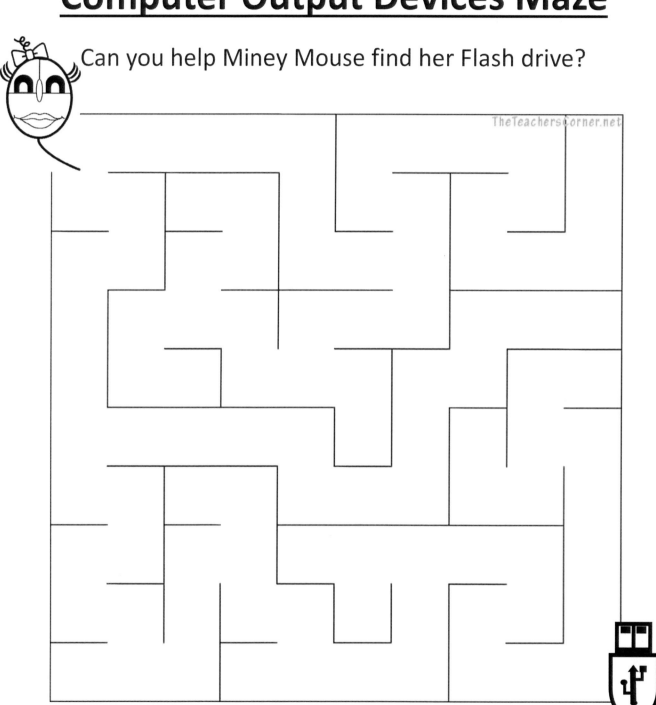

TheTeachersCorner.net

Microsoft Office Tools
Unit 6

Name: _____ Date: _____

Microsoft Office

Draw a line from the icon to the correct program.

Microsoft Outlook

Microsoft Word

Microsoft Excel

Microsoft Publisher

<u>Computer – Microsoft Home Tab</u>

	Office		Print
	New		Publish
	Open		Close
	Save		Copy
	Save As		Cut
	Send		Paste
	Convert		Change Case

Name: _____ Date: _____

Computer – Microsoft Home Tab

	Bullets		Bold
	Numbering		Italics
	Clear All Formatting		Highlight
	Font Color		Left align
	Font Size		Right align
Calibri (Body)	Font Style		Center
	Underline		Justify

Microsoft Word Home Tab

Color the picture of the **_open_** icon below.

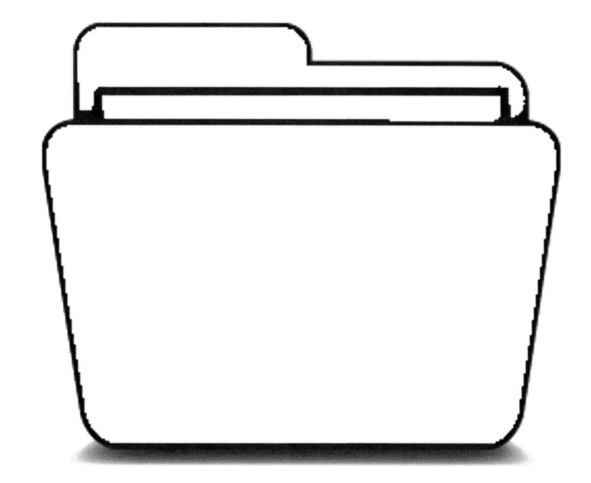

Name: _____ Date: _____

Microsoft Office Word Home Tab

Color the picture of the *save* icon below.

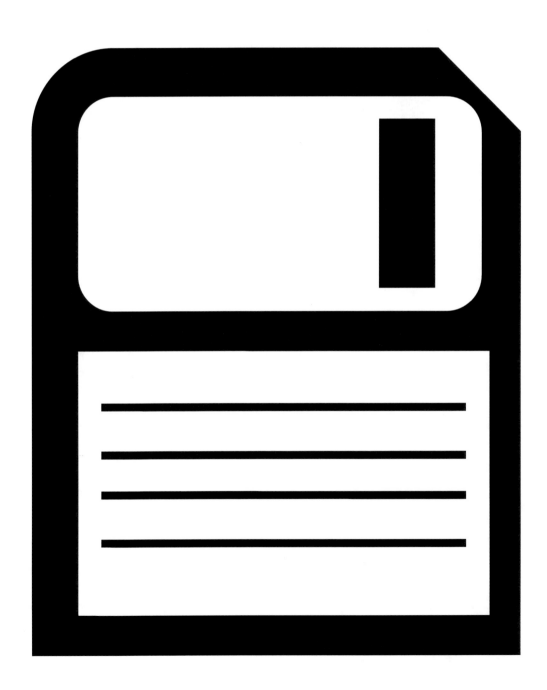

Name: _____ Date: _____

Microsoft Office Word Home Tab

Color the picture of the *cut* icon below.

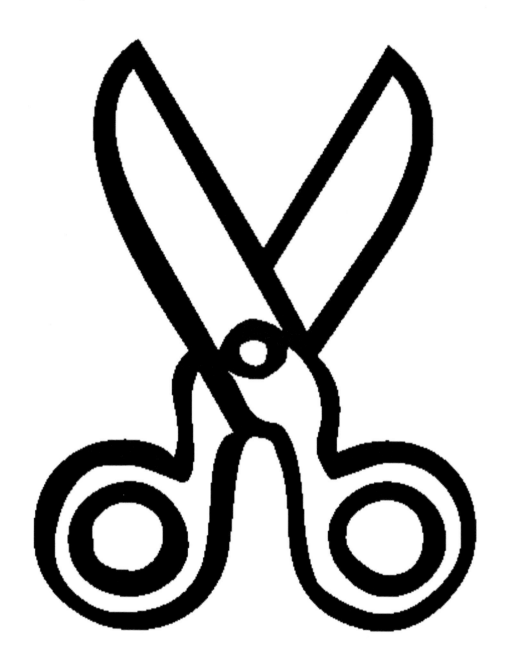

Name: _____ Date: _____

Microsoft Office Word Home Tab

Color the picture of the **copy** icon below.

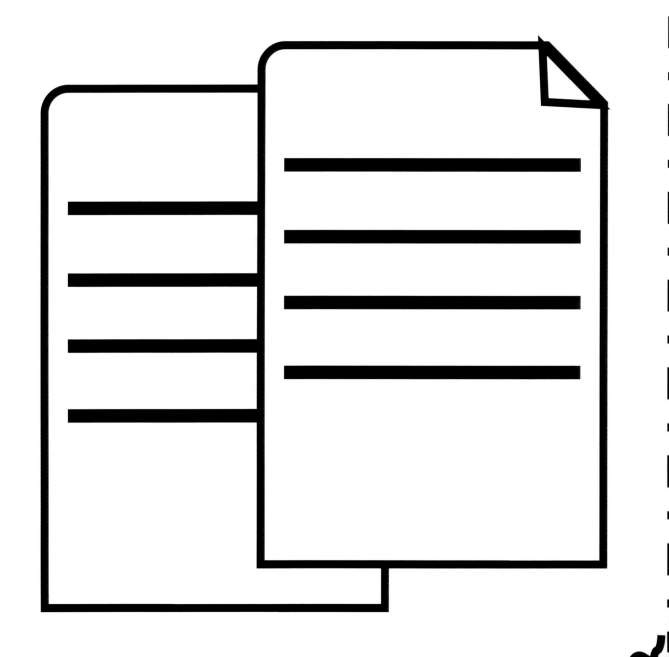

Microsoft Office Word Home Tab

Color the picture of the **paste** icon below.

Storage Devices Word Search

```
E  X  R  G  G  F  C  R  C  O
W  E  N  R  D  L  Y  V  T  X
M  J  T  A  H  R  P  P  S  M
P  M  Z  A  J  A  O  L  M  O
X  N  N  K  S  S  C  W  N  J
O  L  L  T  G  E  X  A  W  Z
H  K  E  V  V  M  V  G  W  S
L  I  M  A  C  E  T  U  C  F
Q  J  S  V  W  B  T  E  F  T
Z  L  R  H  A  O  W  H  N  F
```

SAVE	COPY	PASTE
CUT	NEW	WORD

Processing Device Unit 7

Name: _____ Date: _____

CPU (Central Processing Unit)

- The CPU is the brains of your computer. It processes everything.

- Color the picture of the CPU below.

Name: _____ Date: _____

Processing Device Word Search

```
N  X  R  D  P  T  H  O  A  D
H  O  W  K  L  G  V  M  G  O
M  O  T  H  E  R  B  O  A  D
S  I  P  L  L  A  W  G  K  U
L  N  P  A  O  P  B  K  C  N
L  T  T  R  F  H  L  O  B  I
S  E  K  T  G  I  W  Z  Z  T
V  L  N  N  V  C  P  S  S  U
T  I  W  E  N  S  G  X  Y  V
P  R  O  C  E  S  S  I  N  G
```

CENTRAL   **PROCESSING**   **UNIT**

MOTHERBOAD   **GRAPHICS**   **INTEL**

Name: _____ Date: _____

Computer Processing Device Maze

Can you help Miney Mouse find her CPU?

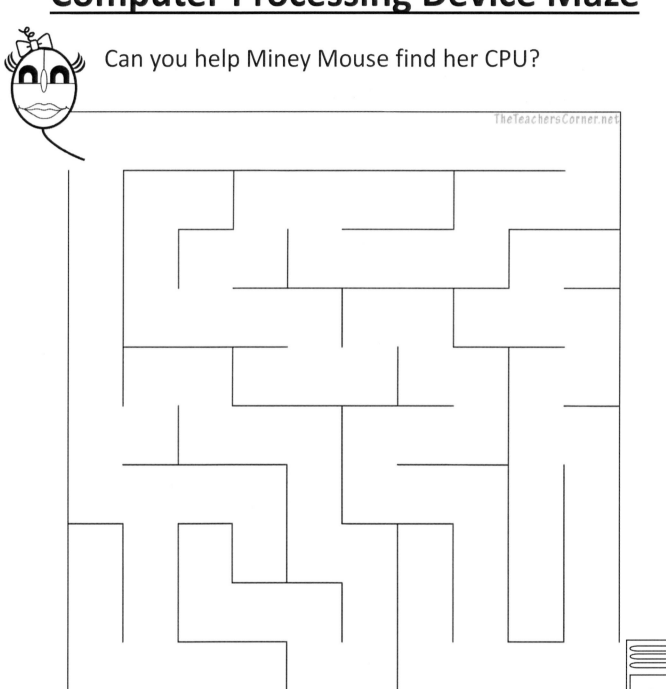

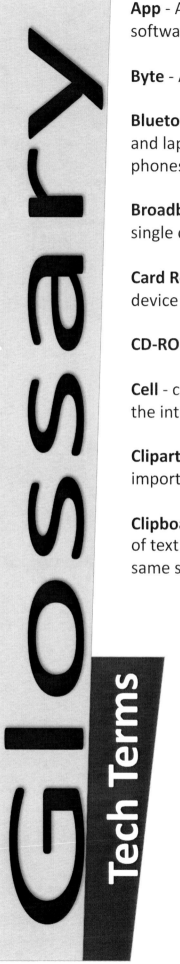

App - App is short for "application," which is the same thing as a software program.

Byte - A byte is a unit of measurement used to measure data.

Bluetooth- It is used for short-range connections between desktop and laptop computers, PDAs, digital cameras, scanners, cellular phones, and printers.

Broadband- This refers to high-speed data transmission in which a single cable can carry a large amount of data at once.

Card Reader -"Card reader" is the generic term for an input device that reads flash memory cards.

CD-ROM - Stands for "Compact Disc Read-Only Memory."

Cell - cell is a specific location within a spreadsheet and is defined by the intersection of a row and column.

Clipart - Clip art is a collection of pictures or images that can be imported into a document or another program.

Clipboard– The clipboard acts as a type of storage area when a piece of text is temporarily removed and stored for later use within the same session.

Copy - Many software programs allow you to copy data, such as text in Microsoft Word.

Desktop - When you boot up your computer, the desktop is displayed once the startup process is complete.

Escape - The Escape key is located in the upper-left corner of a computer keyboard.

Filename - Every file stored on a computer's hard disk has a filename that helps identify the file within a given folder.

Firewall - It acts as a barrier between a trusted system or network and outside connections, such as the Internet.

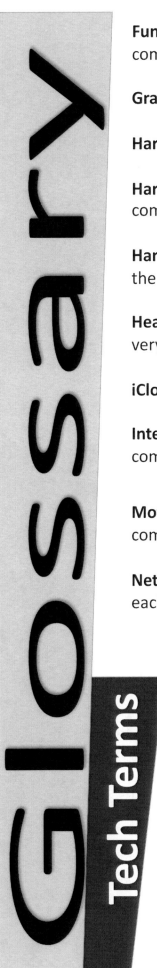

Function - A function key is one of the "F" keys along the top of a computer keyboard.

Graphic - A graphic is an image.

Hard Copy - A hard copy is a printed document.

Hard Disk - When you save data or install programs on your computer, the information is typically written to your hard disk.

Hard Drive - The hard drive is what stores all your data. It houses the hard disk, where all your files and folders are physically located.

Header – The header is similar to a footer except that it sits at the very top of every page in a document.

iCloud - iCloud is an online service provided by Apple.

Internet - The Internet is a global wide area network that connects computer systems across the world.

Motherboard - The motherboard is the main circuit board of your computer and is also known as the mainboard or logic board.

Network - When you have two or more computers connected to each other, you have a network.

Operating System - An operating system, or "OS," is software that communicates with the hardware and allows other programs to run.

Paste - Paste is a command that allows you to insert data from the clipboard into an application.

PDF - Stands for "Portable Document Format.

Power Supply - A power supply is a hardware component that supplies power to an electrical device.

Power Supply - A power supply is a hardware component that supplies power to an electrical device.

PowerPoint - is often used to create business presentations.

Processor - A processor, or "microprocessor," is a small chip that resides in computers and other electronic devices. Its basic job is to receive input and provide the appropriate output.

QR Code - A QR code (short for "quick response" code) is a type of barcode that contains a matrix of dots.

Read Only - A read-only file or storage device contains data that cannot be modified or deleted.

Recycle Bin - When you delete a file or folder in Windows, it is placed in the Recycle Bin.

Spellcheck - is a feature included with various operating systems and applications that checks text for spelling errors.

Sound Card - The sound card is a component inside the computer that provides audio input and output capabilities.

Spreadsheet - A spreadsheet is a document that stores data in a grid of horizontal rows and vertical columns.

Spyware - This is software that "spies" on your computer.

Start Menu - The Start menu is a feature of the Windows operating system that provides quick access to programs, folders, and system settings.

Streaming - Data streaming, commonly seen in the forms of audio and video streaming, is when a multimedia file can be played back without being completely downloaded first.

Text Box - A text box is a rectangular area on the screen where you can enter text.

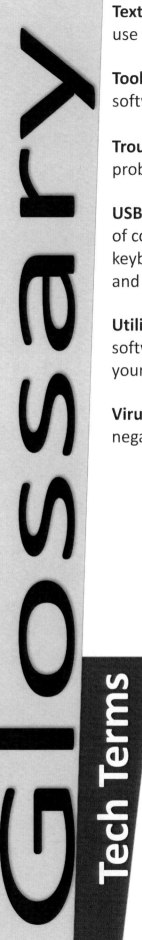

Text Editor - A text editor is any word processing program that you can use to type and edit text.

Toolbar - A toolbar is a set of icons or buttons that are part of a software program's interface or an open window.

Troubleshooting - is the process of identifying the source of a problem.

USB - Stands for "Universal Serial Bus." USB is the most common type of computer port used in today's computers. It can be used to connect keyboards, mice, game controllers, printers, scanners, digital cameras, and removable media drives, just to name a few.

Utility - Utility programs, commonly referred to as just "utilities," are software programs that add functionality to your computer or help your computer perform better.

Virus - Computer viruses are small programs or scripts that can negatively affect the health of your computer.

References

Blaise Pascal Versailles.JPG [Photograph] By Français : anonyme; une copie d'une peinture de François II Quesnel gravée par Gérard Edelinck en 1691. English: unknown; a copy of the painture of François II Quesnel, which was made for Gérard Edelinck en 1691. Polski: nieznany; kopia obrazu Françoisa II Quesnela wykonanego dla Gérarda Edelincka w 1691. (Own work) [GFDL (http://www.gnu.org/copyleft/fdl.html) or CC BY 3.0 (http://creativecommons.org/licenses/by/3.0)], via Wikimedia Commons

CharlesBabbage.jpg [Photograph] By Unknown staff artist for The Illustrated London News [Public domain], via Wikimedia Commons

Gottfried Wilhelm Leibniz c1700.jpg {[Photograph] German Johann Friedrich Wentzel [Public domain], via Wikimedia Commons

IBM Blue Gene P supercomputer.jpg [Photograph] By Argonne National Laboratory's Flickr page [CC BY-SA 2.0 (http://creativecommons.org/licenses/by-sa/2.0)], via Wikimedia Commons

Joe D, Difference Engine[Photograph] (Own work) [CC BY-SA 1.0 (http://creativecommons.org/licenses/by-sa/1.0)], via Wikimedia Commons

Joseph Marie Jacquard.jpg[Photograph] https://commons.wikimedia.org/wiki/File:Joseph_Marie_Jacquard.jpg#file

Made in United States
North Haven, CT
12 August 2022